MIME: LANGUAGE OF THE HEART
Pantomime Acting, Skit Production
And Troupe Formation Principles

By Alexandra McGee

Alexandra McGee (Mime Teacher and Director)
and Dennis McGee (Producer)
of the Heartbeatmime Troupe

TABLE OF CONTENTS

CHAPTER 1: The Forming of a Mime Troupe
CHAPTER 2: Principles of Mime Acting
CHATER 3: Exercises for Learning Mime
CHAPTER 4: Practice and Performance
CHAPTER 5: Make up and Costume

CHAPTER 1

The Forming of a Mime Troupe

The purpose of this book is to help those who either aspire to do or teach pantomime. With a minimal amount of theater background, you can learn the gentle art of mime that speaks directly to the heart of the observer by studying the 12 principles in this book and in the skits on the ""doveinturkey"" account on YouTube. There also are step by step instructions on how to form a mime troupe. By applying the principles and the practice and performance guidelines you can have a troupe that wows your typical street audience.

Mime is its own art, not just theater without words. I hope you will be one of those who, like Marcel Marceau, can speak across language, cultural and religious barriers directly to the greatest concerns of the heart.

Marcel Marceau called mime "the language of the heart" because it telescopes story to motivations and feelings that underlie human life. Mime speaks to the common man. It gives a message about desires, important events of life, character choices and humorous predicaments. It doesn't provide an immediate solution for an imperfect world, nor pretend to effect immediate change on the society. But it does plant seeds of thought and feeling in fertile soil, so that anyone watching will have something to meditate on, something to take home and apply to their own life.

This book is based on my experiences while training sixty-plus young people in eight mime troupes, who have performed in four countries, on three continents. Our first mime troupe consisted of my five teenage kids and two young men. One fellow was an engineer, the other a banker. They had taken their vacations in the summer of 2008 to come and learn mime from me. If they could do it, so can you!

These are the main qualifications I look for in a prospective mime:

- A desire to interact with others graciously – you can't be a loner or a dictator in a mime troupe.
- Between the ages of fifteen and thirty. I have made exceptions on the younger end, but it is always a bit difficult. There is a maturity level needed to deal with disappointment at a practice, or not getting a part you want. Also there is a concentration level needed that younger kids often don't have. As for adults who are older than thirty, we found that it was harder for them to learn with the same retention, ease and stamina as younger students. The audience is quicker to forgive any amateurism in young adults whom they know are enjoying the mime as a lark.
- Artistic talent. I put this last, because although talent is necessary to be able to learn how to mime, the first two qualities are even more necessary; without them the troupe will not be able to work together smoothly. When mime is done in a troupe, you can have small parts and big parts. The small parts I give to those who are not as flexible physically or agile in their acting repertoire. If they have a good attitude and don't mind having small "helper" parts – that are very much needed in a mime play – then they can be a great asset to the troupe.

Mime is more challenging than many theater arts, because it has the double requirement of strength like a ballerina and acting skills like an actor. Five to ten mimes is the ideal number for a troupe, although I did use twenty mimes to stage a Christmas play.

These are the specific roles that need assigning in a mime troupe:
1) Director – one who can teach and demonstrate the principles. Beginners in mime need someone who can observe a whole skit from the audience's perspective.
2) Assistant Director(s) –An assistant will take a play that the director has already presented to the mimes and he will direct the mimes, who are in that particular skit, during a practice. Part of the practice time is spent breaking up into two or three groups who are practicing their particular skits.
3) Mimes – have good learner attitudes, are gracious towards others, between ages of fifteen and thirty and like to have fun!

CHAPTER 2

The Principles of Mime

I have identified twelve principles of Mime. Four of them are expression principles, while eight are movement principles. I teach them in order of complexity: the first principles being the most basic ones that every mime should know. The last four principles are more difficult and only those with a natural ability and eagerness to grow will be able to master them.

<u>12 Principles of Mime</u>

1. Wonder/Wisdom
2. Thought, Thought, Thought
3. Looney Tuneys
4. Counterpoint
5. Isolation
6. Clicks
7. Echoes
8. Fidelity
9. Phrasing and Freezes
10. Mime Time
11. Motivation
12. Character Growth

Principle #1 - Mime Expression: Wonder/Wisdom

Mime skits have an underlying theme of discovery. This is partly because, as there are no or few props or scenery, the mime has to help you discover the story primarily through his actions and expressions.

In order then to effectively express the reality of the objects, situation or feelings, the mime must have an intensity of interaction in the scene that is most like the wonder of a child who comes upon something new to him, or the wisdom of an older person who is sharing with you something precious and valuable.

Another reason for the wonder or wisdom characteristic of the mime can be found in the life and philosophy of Marcel Marceau.

> "Marcel Marceau was the legendary mime, who survived the Nazi occupation, and saved many children in WWII. He was regarded for his peerless style pantomime, moving audiences without uttering a single word, and was known to the World as a "master of silence." … At the beginning of the Second World War, he had to hide his Jewish origin and changed his name to Marceau, when his Jewish family was forced to flee their home. His father was deported to Auschwitz, where he was killed in 1944. Both Marceau and his brother, Alain, were in the French underground, helping children to escape to safety in neutral Switzerland. Then Marceau served as

interpreter for the Free French Forces under General Charles de Gaulle, acting as liaison officer with the allied armies ... In the early 1950s, he was virtually unknown in his native France (which has a strong mime tradition). Laurel & Hardy were doing a world tour, and while they were playing in Paris, someone tipped them off that Marceau was doing incredible mime in an insignificant suburban theatre. They went to see him, and, ... a few days later ... during ... their regular show, after the Interval, Stan introduced Marceau ... scolded the audience for ignoring such a talent... and then Laurel & Hardy walked offstage and gave the second half of their show to Marceau."

Found at IMBD, Marcel Marceau bio.

Marceau died at 84 on Sept. 24, 2007. It was reading a tribute to Marceau's life that triggered my husband's idea for our family to learn and perform mime.

Mime presents a childlike discovery of the pathos or humor of the human condition. Without a childlike commentary on human life that becomes wisdom because it was learned in innocence, mime becomes mere clowning or illusionism or critical theatre that will not touch the heart in a gracious manner.

Principle #2 - Mime Expression: Thought, Thought, Thought

I learned a wonderful exercise at The School of Modern Mime in Warsaw from the professional mime Ewelina Ciszewska called "Yes, No, Yes!" The whole troupe circles around each other like an Indian war dance. You stomp for each word: Yes! No! Yes! The first yes and no are smaller stomps, almost hesitant. The yes is directed toward the other mimes, the no turns away from the circle of mimes and more to oneself. The last Yes! is a big stomp that then seeks to face another mime in the group. This is then repeated a dozen times in order to get the mimes used to a rhythm of positive, negative, positive.

An example of how this works in mime acting would be how Adam and Eve responded to the offer of the apple. They say "Yes" at first, because they know they have free will that God gave them to obey Him or not. Adam and Eve forget that they are giving up in relationship with God. They then turn away with a "No", because they remember that God told them not to eat it. But then again they turn back to the snake and say "Yes" to the apple. This decision for consumption of the shiny, red, glossy apple marks the human race's separation from God and the destruction of the world.

The goal of the exercise is not actual interaction with another mime, but rather the inner drama of thought behind the individual mime's action. Really you want to say yes, and at first you do … but you are not sure that yes is acceptable, you are not sure it is the best course, you are not sure you can do it, you are not sure if it is dangerous – there are many reasons why you don't stick to your first Yes right away. The final yes is emphatic because you have decided to take that route. Of course it can also be the reverse, "No. Yes. No!"

The Yes, No, Yes exercise pinpoints the moment of thought that precedes the completion of an action, or the thoughts between actions. Although a mime may not do this with every single action, it should be the common thought before doing anything profound on the stage. Mime is meant to play with ideas, not just suggest invisible objects.

Besides "Yes. No. Yes!" before an action, the mime is to have a wave of thought and emotions during and after the movement (not silent mouthing of words or making childish faces) as well. As Gregg Goldstone, another mime performer and instructor at the Warsaw School of Modern Mime, would say, "Don't hurry to get 'There.' There is no 'There.' " By this he meant that hurried mime movement and suggestion (showing invisible objects) is not good mime. There needs to be thought shown before, during and after each movement. Using the steps above, the thought becomes complex rather than too simple.

There can be a particular movement or expression the mime makes that sets off this conflicted thought; then every time the mime makes that particular movement or expression, the audience is drawn into the conflict again. An example of this occurs in our "Unmasked" skit that you can watch at our website Heartbeatmime.com. A script of the skit can also be found at the Heartbeatmime.com website. Every time a mime takes off his mask, he then gives expression to his inner pain or lack of love. This trigger (of taking off the masks) communicates to the audience that there will now be a revelation of the inner life.

For a scene to have humor or pathos, the story has to have progressed to a point that the audience understands conflicting motives in the mime. An example of this could be when a mime is offered an ice cream by another mime who has enjoyed another ice cream in front of the first mime. The first mime refuses because he doesn't want to look too eager, but his eyes show that he really wants the ice cream.

Principle #3 – Mime Movement: Looney Tuneys

Looney Tuneys but Cheaper

With mime you can be one inch high in a field of blueberry bushes, or you can be a giant in a land of tiny people, you can fly south with the geese, or swim with the whales. Without props and without scenery, however, it is necessary that the body and expression of the mime be large enough so that the audience, often sitting or standing at least six feet away, can see what you are doing. For this reason, everything a mime does must be huge.

Like a cartoon character, the mime needs to take up the space he stands on as well as all the space in a Looney Tuneys sphere surrounding him. Looney Tuneys movements are bigger than a natural movement. Actions and expressions are exaggerated, not like a satirist or a clown, but large enough for Aunt Myrtle in the back row, or the passing kid listening to his i-pod, to notice out of the corner of his eyes.

Looney Tuneys facial expression:

Looney Tuneys expression begins in the eyes. They are large because the thoughts are large. Think loud thoughts and show your feelings in your eyes. The rest of your face will follow. Some mimes need to specifically work on widening the eyes. Large eyes filled with feeling are very compelling and help the audience see into the soul. Expressive eyebrows and forehead can adorn those feelings, but don't let them substitute for the emotion coming from the eyes of the mime.

The mime needs to fluctuate between large obvious thoughts and large subtle thoughts. This is a form of counterpoint that is discussed in the next section. But I want to emphasize here that even subtle thoughts are expressed in a big way, through the use of dead-pan expression, with maybe only the lifting of an eyebrow or the tilt of a head. It is important to allow these more subtle expressions to be interspersed in a mime's performance. The variety helps highlight the intense moments and gives comic relief to the audience between those moments.

Early in our family's exploration of mime, my son would have his mouth open wide in a kind of perpetual wonder of every situation. I kept telling him to close his mouth, to only have it slightly open, with the innocence of a child. He listened and eventually mastered some of the more intricate and deep emotional expressions because he knew how to be subtle as well as intense.

<u>Looney Tuneys and Bigger than Life:</u>

Just as the cartoon characters fill up the screen and do movements that are bigger than life, so the mime needs to stand tall. He needs to straighten his spine, as if it were suspended from above, hold his head high, and project his chest. His hips and legs should be firm and somewhat tensed toward the audience, as if to say, "I am here! Look at me!" The mime is to have a solid stage presence, firmly grounded on the stage but with energy and strength, ready for whatever adventure befalls.

I am always telling my mimes that their whole body must be involved in every movement. In every movement, from taking a gun out of his pocket and putting it to his head, to taking a heart out of his chest and offering it to a sad soul, the mime must move with energy from the tip of his head to his toes. The whole body must have energy and tension.

When moving, be sure the whole body moves in some kind of way along with the primary movement. Think of how tennis players use their whole body to reach a ball, not just the arm with the racket. Similarly, mimes express with their whole body the energy that is used by the arm or leg or neck or face to act. The worst mime skits I've seen have so-called mimes, who move their bodies just as they do in their natural life, just without words.

Looney Tuneys and Objects:

I mentioned earlier that suggested objects are often extensions of the character. Mime objects must also often be larger than life. This is so that Aunt Myrtle in the back row can see it. At the same time the mime's body will take on some of the characteristics of the object. For example, when playing the violin, the mime's hips may sway echoing (a principle we will talk more about later) the rounded curves of the violin and the full sound. The bow arm will sometimes be round and smooth (and larger than what it takes to play a real violin) and sometimes hard and choppy. If a mime is holding a box, his body will be rigid and box-like. If he is holding a furry cat, the mime's movements will be soft and gentle like the cat, unless of course the cat scratches, then the mime's reaction is harsh and violent.

Looney Tuneys and Characterization:

In one skit that I performed in class at the School of Modern Mime, I was a cat that was not happy to be treated like a dumb dog. The skit ended with the master throwing a ball for the cat to "fetch". The cat looks at the ball with some interest, then disinterest, then looks at the master, casually looks away (notice the thought, thought, thought,) and then holds up his paw (fingers curved down) and then shows, like a jack-knife, as Jerry might in the Tom and Jerry cartoons, each individual claw of his paw: 1! 2! 3! 4! 5! This way the audience gets a view of the evil intention of the cat that is more specific than if I had just made my hands like claws down at my sides.

Other Looney Tuneys movements:

When walking toward an object, project over the object. This means to tilt your face to look up and past everything that is on stage. Your viewpoint should be to the top of the heads of the people in the back row. Otherwise your face will be facing down too much for the audience to be able to see it. If you must look at down at the floor, you may glance, but mostly let your eyeballs look down, don't tilt your face. The audience needs to be able to see the emotions on your face.

Mimes don't dance or jump. Mimes do a partial lift off from the feet. The heel of the feet will rise along with the arch, but the balls of the feet stay on the floor. Mimes always maintain their presence on the floor. They do not habitually go on their tippy toes, nor jump as a ballerina might. Of course there are exceptions – but exceptions are no longer exceptions if they are found in every skit you perform.

In a jump rope skit we perform, the mime's feet remain firmly on the ground. When the mime's arms go up, it shows that the rope is going up; the mime at the same time bends his knees, so that his body goes down. When his arms come back down, swinging the suggested (invisible) rope under his feet, his legs straighten and so his body goes up, suggesting a jump in the air. This gives the illusion of jumping while his feet stay on the ground.

Bring everything you can front and center stage. If, for example, you are suggesting a wall, let it be right in between you and the audience. They can see through it. And they will get to see all the emotions on your face.

Don't hold your breath, close your eyes or cross your arms. We want to see all of you and experience all of your presence. Don't close off to the audience.

Always move in a stylized manner. Each movement needs to be sharp and clear with a definite start and finish. The mime is a cross between a doll and a robot; he is emotional as dolls might be, but robotic in his lack of fluid or mushy human movement.

Principle #4 – Mime movement: Counterpoint

Counterpoint in Thoughts and Feelings

Counterpoint runs through every aspect of mime movement and expression. It has already been discussed in the section on thought with the exercise "Yes, No, Yes". Because there is no dialogue, the contrast between a positive and negative emotional response helps the audience understand what is being thought through by the mime. Therefore, it is a good idea to preface a major emotion with its opposite.

Physical Counterpoint

Physical counterpoint is used to show the mime's place in relation to suggested (invisible) objects, such as when leaning on a suggested wall or table. The mime must enable the audience to "see" the contrast between air and suggested (invisible) solid objects. Physical counterpoint movement makes those objects "real". This is necessary because of the minimal props and scenery on the mime stage.

The mime performs physical counterpoint when he moves one part of his body in the reverse or opposite direction of the suggested object. If the object is high (for instance, looking up at a tall mountain) the mime will bend his knees and go low. If the object is low (like a jump rope that is going under our feet) the mime will go high, into a "raised onto the balls of the feet" position. When hands are placed on an object (on a wall, for example) the mime's body will shift to the side, while keeping his hand on the same spot of the wall, to show the placement of the wall.

To suggest effort or energy, the mime must push or pull in the opposite direction. For example, in the Tug-of-War skit, the mimes have their arms stretched toward their opponent to suggest that they are pulling on the rope, but at the same time they have their backs and heads leaning back away from the mime who is pulling on the other side. This gives the illusion of pulling with extreme effort. You can see our Tug-of-War skit at our website, Heartbeatmime.com as well as download a script.

Counterpoint when handling objects

When approaching an object to touch it, there are two possible forms of counterpoint that the mime must do.

First he will slightly back away from the object, as if the energy of the object creates a force field that pushes him way from it.

Then he will approach. In order to touch the object his hand will first form a shape that is the opposite of the shape of the object. Then his hand will assume the shape of the object, wrapping around it or pressing against it, in order to reveal it to the audience.

For example, when approaching a suggested (invisible) wall, the hand will be slightly cup-shaped, curved, as if holding a baseball, in opposition to the flat wall. Then the hand will flatten out as the palm touches the wall. When leaving the wall, the hand will curve again, as it leaves the wall, to show that it is no longer on the wall.

When suggesting a long wall, the mime will place one hand on the wall and then a second hand. (This is done one at a time because of the principle of isolation, that is explained later in this book.) To move along a wall, the mime lifts and places one hand at a time, leading with the hand that is in the direction he wishes to move. Between each hand lift and placement, he moves his body a step in that direction as well. It is important that the hands are fixed in the air on the same spot (on the invisible wall) while his body moves. Then the audience will see the solidity of the wall. This is shown in our skit "In My Place" on my "doveinturkey" account at YouTube. A script of the skit can be found at the Heartbeatmime.com website.

When approaching an apple, the hand will be flat, in contrast to the apple. The hand will then cup (with a "click"– a principle explained later) over the apple. When setting the apple down, the hand will change into a flattened position as it draws away from the apple, to make clear it is no longer holding the apple.

All bodily movements will have hints of counterpoint in them for a mime. For example, if a mime offers something (perhaps with two hands – as this Looney Tuneys movement shows more commitment and sincerity)- one of his feet may point out in the opposite direction, like what a ballerina does. A mime will not be quite as exaggerated as a ballerina, but enough to give the audience the impression of an arrow of energy going from his toe toward his outstretched hands. The body will be slightly leaning to show this flow of energy as well.

<u>Counterpoint and Environment</u>

Counterpoint is useful also for revealing weather. The mime must first show the opposite of what he wants to show is there. If you have a skit where it is raining, start with no rain and then have a few drops at a time, each drop causing a slight bob of the body or head as the mime feels them. The drops slowly speed up until you have a downpour with the person pulling up his collar, putting his newspaper over his head and running off the stage.

Principle #5 – Mime Movement: Isolation

Since the audience sees only body movements and emotions of the mimes, these are very important for the intelligibility of the skit. Each movement or facial expression must move forward the plot of the skit and needs to be showcased. For this reason the mime needs to emphasize the body part that is most important for each mime movement and he needs to downplay movement in the rest of his body. This doesn't mean, of course, that the rest of his body isn't doing counterpoint as previously taught, but the other body parts will not be doing something totally different. For example, a mime would not sit down and at the same time open a suggested newspaper with his hands. The mime is somewhat like a robot, which only moves one limb at a time, but with added feeling, emotion and thought.

    Using isolation means the mime intentionally moves isolated parts of the body one at a time. This doesn't mean that the rest of the body is limp, but that there is only one part of the body doing anything that moves the plot forward. The rest of the body supports the primary movement or expression with posture, energy and counterpoint to the primary movement. The rest of the body may even echo a primary movement, but only after the primary movement has happened. In this way it brings more attention or emphasis to the primary movement and eliminates distraction from the main body part that is moving.

    An example of this can be seen on our "doveinturkey" account on YouTube in the skit entitled "It is Better to Give than Get." The script can be found at the Heartbeatmime.com website. When the children are tying their balloons, they have their hands stretched out in front of them. They tie/twist the string onto the mouth of the balloon. The index finger and thumb are doing the twisting, while the other three fingers are splayed out into the air. This magnifies the tying. The rest of their bodies are quite still so as not to distract from the balloon tying.

The first time an action is seen it may need to be repeated to be sure that it is understood. Also, it is often slower than real-time to allow the audience time to process what is happening. The next two times will be quicker than real-life speed. Since the audience now understands what the action represents, this abbreviation is possible with no loss of comprehension. Generally no action should be repeated more than three of four times or the audience may lose interest.

Another application of isolation is that there cannot be diverse actions performed by different mimes at the same time on the stage, otherwise the audience may lose track of the plot. They will not know which action to follow or which is the primary action. If several of the mimes are all doing exactly the same action at the same time this is okay. This adds comedy and emphasizes the action. For example in the skit, "It is Better to Give than Get," two of the children tie their balloons at the same time. Their motions are synchronized.

Principle #6 – Mime Movement: Clicks

Clicks are what give the biggest artistic punch to mime. Clicks in the mime's movement give the appearance of being in an old movie – you know the kind that flickered all the time. The clicks at the end of each movement create an illusion similar to still photographs in succession. These clicks are valuable in mime because they give the audience a moment to register the movement that just happened before they move on to the next movement.

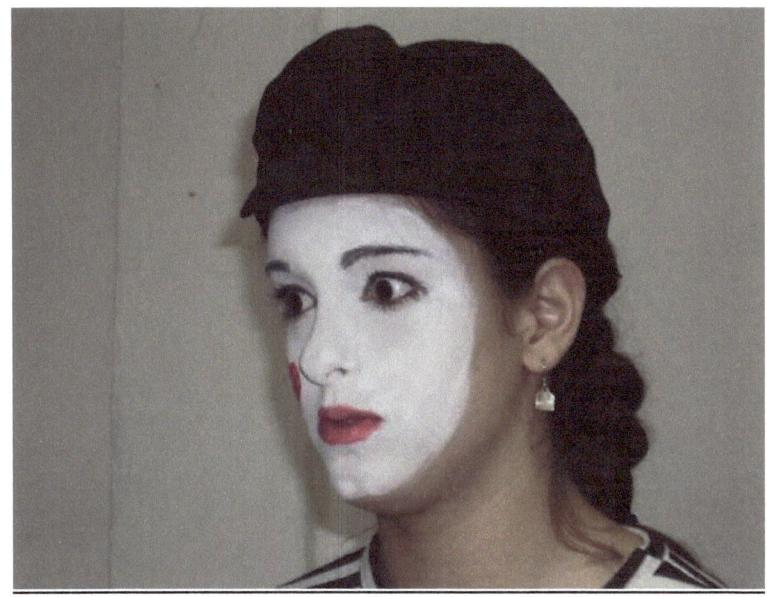

Clicks when interacting with objects

Also, when suggesting objects, a click allows the mime to show the physical presence of the object. For example, as a mime picks a (suggested) flower from the ground, he will pluck and have a short click (sudden stop of movement) before bringing his hand up to his face to smell the pretty flower. This click upon plucking the flower suggests that there was an effort to pull the stalk and a point in time when it broke off into his hand.

Whole body clicks to indicate change of direction or purpose:

In dramatic theater, the actor flows between feelings, often overlapping feeling with movement, dialogue and interaction with props. The mime, in contrast, must have staccato / snapshot movements so that the audience can discern the different feelings that are not expressed in words and can see the objects that are not visible to the eye. Clicks are even more pronounced when they are at the beginning or end of movements of the torso. This is because a change of direction of the torso should be indicating a change of intention. This click of the whole body is like an impulse that begins in the gut, diaphragm or chest. Then the rest of the body follows this click into movement.

Principle #7 – Mime Movement: Echoes

Just as in a good play script or movie screenplay, there needs to be smooth interaction between the actors or the mimes. Each mime can't express himself independently, separate from the rest of the group, or the audience will lose a sense of cohesion and emotional power in the skit.

There is always a leader, one person who is doing the primary movement at any given moment; the other mimes can provide echoes for him. If mimes other than the main character are moving, they should be providing an echo that draws attention back to the character that is moving the plot forward.

There are times when some mimes in the skit cannot add anything to the character currently taking the lead. In this case the other mimes may freeze, rather than provide some kind of echo. But any time mimes are interacting together, the supporting mimes need to move in such a way as to enhance the lead mime's movements.

The echo might just be a sympathetic lean toward, or a standoffish lean away from the mime, or it might be an actual imitation of the primary mime's actions. Finally, the mimes on the stage must have an eye toward spatial relations that keeps the audience seeing things in a balanced and symmetrical way.

The Mime Company at Northwestern University has a video on YouTube with many great ideas. Even when their skits have several actors moving at one time, they are careful to echo each other. In the ballerina skit, for example, the boys are all making similar movements of running after the girl, while she is the leader with movements that hit the boys as they try to approach her.

Another impressive performance is their seaweed plant. There the mimes are all echoing each other, being separate branches of one plant, moving with the current of the water. The seaweed representation is an example of Corporal Mime, created by Etienne Decroux. Marcel Marceau studied under Decroux, who is often called the Father of Modern Mime. In Corporeal Mime, the mime characters play the roles of inanimate objects in skin-tight body suit costumes. Echoing is prevalent in Corporeal Mime. The movement is more like dance than Marceau's style of mime; there is less emphasis on plot. Marceau characterized his mime as story-oriented. In the skits my troupes have performed, the echoing is usually more subtle than in Corporeal Mime, but contributes to the harmony and beauty of the story.

Occasionally I have a group movement, as in the "The Trap" skit, where all the evil temptations (who are mimes) push the man into the box. They are not actually touching the man, but in several layers around and over him their hands pulse the air and give the illusion of pushing him into the box. Of course, the mime is slowly lowering himself at the same rate as the other mimes are pushing him down.

In our mime it is rare to actually touch another mime; we do it only in exceptional situations, like when a mime falls backward like a stiff board and is caught by another mime (as in the skit "Unmasked"). Echoes show the interaction or influence between mimes, but without physical contact.

Principle #8 Mime Movement: Fidelity

Fidelity to the reality of invisible things is important in mime so that the audience doesn't lose track of what is happening. If an object is set down, and then the mime walks through it, the audience will feel cheated, as if they were lied to about that object and it isn't really there.

There is a mime on YouTube called "The Audition" by tomanddave.com in which the mime shows fidelity to invisible objects even after the non-mime "director" in the skit has asked the mime to stop doing whatever silly thing he is doing with his suggested objects. The mime is thus interrupted several times by the "director" during his mime audition because he keeps talking. So he puts away the hanging ladder, finds a key he has thrown away earlier, wipes a smudge on his suggested machine and moves a suggested box out of the way. This provides much of the humor of the sketch.

Principle #9 – Mime Movement: Phrases and Freezes

    A phrase in mime is like a sentence in dialogue. For example, "Look at this pretty flower I'm holding!" is a phrase. It will likely contain two to five movements. In this example the mime could first hold the flower out and show wonder in his face, then bring it close to his face and smell its divine aroma, and finally hold it in front of himself and tilt his head to look at it admiringly.

    Each of these movements have started and stopped with a click (as described above). But the phrase also has a definite ending – it is called a freeze. It is slightly longer than a click, but not as emphatic. The freeze helps the audience to know that that a statement has been made. Then they are ready for the next phrase (series of movements that express a sentence of thought).

    During the freeze, the mime will have an emotional response to the phrase he just expressed. The mime needs to make each change of thought and emotion clear and not blurry or fuzzy, so that the audience can read what is happening. The "thought, thought, thought" that happens at the beginning, during and end of phrases is what helps the audience to truly understand and empathize with the mime. That is why the body needs to pause so that the audience can focus on the mime's face that is thinking thoughts, rather than on his body that is moving. The freezes at the end of phrases will slow down the mime skit slightly, but there is no rush to get "there". Every three to four seconds the mime might express a new phrase, with a freeze at the end.

Principle #10 – Mime Movement: Mime Time

Bartlomiej Ostapczuk (a terrific Polish mime and instructor at the Warsaw School of Modern Mime) called it being "Off the Clock". Mime Time means that the mime almost never acts in real time. Some things he will do quicker than real life, others will be in slow motion. An example of these two different mime times can be seen in our skit "Peace" that is on the "doveinturkey" account on YouTube. The script can be found at the Heartbeatmime.com website. In this skit the two mimes first run around in slow motion and then fight, slapping each other in fast motion. There will be variety of rhythm with each phrase and thought, depending on the nature of the thought.

Mime Time also includes stillness. There will be times of stillness that show the mime is thinking. The audience will appreciate these times to catch up with the meaning of the actions as well as the thoughts of the mime.

Mime Time can compress time by doing miniature versions of actions in a fast speed, so that the audience understands that much has just happened in a small segment of space and time. For example, if a mime is opening a present, he will start with looking at the present with wonder and excitement (slower than real time), start to unwrap the bow, perhaps in real time, and then take off the rest of the ribbon and paper in fast speed time with quick short movements. This helps the audience stay interested in actions that move the plot along but are don't have a lot of thought involved in them.

We like to do chase scenes in slow motion because that makes the chase longer without needing a lot of ground to run on. Also a slow motion chase scene allows the audience to see the expressions on the faces of the mimes while they move. Finally, mime time is funny when it is opposite to what is in real life. For example, an old man shuffling along at break-neck speed is funnier than if he is taking a long time to cross the stage. A chase scene that is fast in real life is funny when we can see every frantic move of the mimes clearly in slow motion.

Principle # 11 - Mime Expression: Motivated Expression

The focus of a mime skit is the characters that the mimes portray. There needs to be a goal, desire, conflict or strong feeling in the mime before he begins the plot of his story. When the expression on the face and the energy of the whole body of the mime (in his posture, his walk, his stance, his carriage of his head) expresses this WANT, the object he suggests also has meaning and feeling and the audience cares.

In order to express ideas or emotion, the Mime should not indicate or point with his fingers, nor mouth out words. For mime speaking, the mime should just say, "Ba, ba, ba, ba…" (silently of course). The focus in mime is on plot, action and emotion, not dialogue or props. The audience needs most of all to understand who you are, why you are there and what matters to you.

Although the suggestion of objects, that is the showing of invisible objects, is an intriguing component of mime, it is important to realize that the focus of the mime is people (character and plot development), not objects. When several mimes are performing in a skit the relationships between the characters is the most important component of the skit. When a mime performs solo, it is his character that is the focus of the skit, more than any objects he suggests.

Objects found in the skit are like an overflow of the mime character. They could be thought of as part of the mime's costume (though invisible and suggested) rather than a separate object that the mime will walk up to and show the audience. The best way to indicate objects then is by their use, not by showing their shape or location. This is done when you smell a flower, lean on a table, peek around a wall or bit into an apple; rather than indicating the shapes of petals, tables, walls or apples.

Principle #12 – Mime Expression: Character Growth

The best character-driven stories have heroes and heroines who go through a journey of change. They start out with a goal and with strengths, but also with weaknesses. The mime character will usually start out with a Wonder / Innocence / Naiveté that then turns into Wisdom that he learns through dealing with conflict. Most mime characters, if they are in the style of Marcel Marceau, are likeable. They are often a kind of underdog. The audience feels it can identify with the strong and weak moments of the mime character. The character lets you into the

inner workings of his thoughts and motivations

Each character will identify salient traits early in the skit. Each character has a goal. The main character (and perhaps others) will have obstacles that stop the character from achieving his goal. Often the obstacles are internal ones due to his own weakness. As the character deals with the conflict, he goes through times of thought and "Yes, No, Yes" thinking patterns. Eventually he makes a choice, sometimes under pressure, that attains (or perhaps misses) his goal.

CHAPTER 3
Lessons For Learning Mime

    During our intensive summer mime programs at Heartbeatmime, the new mimes learn from experienced mimes in our troupe. By using assistant directors and placing new mimes in smaller parts at first, I am able to teach enough of the basics of the art of pantomime to prepare new mimes for street performance within two days. Teaching a whole troupe from scratch, however, will take longer if there aren't other mimes who can model the principles.

    Each of the six lessons in this book teaches two principles. I cite online videos that demonstrate each of the principles. I have included solo and group exercises. The "doveinturkey" account on YouTube has skits that we perform with captions where the principles are modeled.

Lesson 1

Principles: 1. Wonder and Wisdom. 2. Thought, Thought, Thought.

YouTube video: City Lights by Charlie Chaplin. (Marcel Marceau considered Charlie Chaplin his role model)

Solo Exercise:

Find an object on the stage (Wonder/Wisdom). Show what the object is by using it in a unique way: bouncing a ball, for example.

Think about the object through several contrasting thoughts and then decide and execute a course of action. Freeze after the action with some conclusion of learned wisdom. (thought, thought, thought – yes, no, yes).

Group Exercise:

In groups of three, one mime will show the other two an object. All three are to negotiate something about the object. The mimes should plan what they will do before performing. Be sure to take turns initiating action. Show wonder and wisdom. Show interest, doubt, further interest.

    Start with all three mimes posed in an interesting position on stage. End in a frozen position. Do this as much as possible for every skit. This is something we are newly incorporating into our mime.

Lesson 2:

Principles: 3. Looney Tuneys 4. Counterpoint

YouTube: Mitchell Evans, The Weightlifter.

A Concert in Pantomime - Bodecker & Neander Silence

Solo Exercise:

Push, pull or carry something heavy across the stage. Suggested objects and movements should be larger than life. Show counterpoint between body parts as well as between consecutive movements.

Group Exercise:

In groups of two, interact on stage in a way that shows counterpoint, as in a tug of war, for example. Interact three times. The first time reveals the conflict to the audience. The second time escalates the conflict. The third time resolves the conflict. Every interaction must be big, cartooney and with counterpoint tension.

Lesson 3:

Principles: 5. Isolation 6. Clicks

YouTube: 8:46 A.M. "A Traditional, Serious Mime Sketch about 9/11" – Beau Chevassuss

Solo Exercise:

Sit on a chair doing office work. Use isolation and clicks. While using the suggested objects, remember to incorporate: 1) wonder at first and wisdom at the end, 2) at least one instance of thought, thought, thought, 3) looney tuney largeness and 4) counterpoint.

Group Exercise:

In groups of three to five, suggest a workplace with manual labor (not office work). Start in frozen poses on the stage. Work together doing different parts of a job. Have only one mime at a time be the focus of attention. Be sure to use clicks and to isolate the body parts that are performing the action. Give the mimes five minutes to plan their sketch beforehand.

Lesson 4:

Principles: 7. Echoes 8. Fidelity

YouTube: Silent Storytelling: The Art of the Mime – Northwestern University Mime and The Audition for a Mime Sketch Show Live – daveandtom.com

Solo Exercise:

Use an object. Put it down. Walk around the stage, then use the object again.

Group Exercise:

In groups of four or five, be a crowd doing something together. One mime is the leader, while everyone else echoes his movements. Example: Watch a tennis match. Play volleyball. Toss and kick and head a ball between people in a circle. Jump rope.

Lesson 5:

Principles: 9. Phrasing and Freezes 10. Mime Time

YouTube: Cool Mime! Tyson Eberly Mime Performance Part 2

Solo Exercises:

Act out a profession (lawyer, doctor or teacher etc) showing several phrases of movement. Be sure to have slight freezes between phrases.

Example: A firefighter rides on a truck, arrives at a fire, hooks up the hose, shoots the water, sees a victim high up, climbs a ladder and gets him down.

Group Exercises:

In groups of three make a skit that has three sections: normal, slow motion and fast motion. Be sure to incorporate the other principles as well.

Example:

1. *normal time*: two mimes are swimming around
2. *slow motion*: one of the mimes starts drowning and is rescued by the third mime
3. *fast motion*: the mimes happily congratulate each other when the drowning mime spits out water and wakes up.

Lesson 6:

Principles: 9. Motivation 10. Character Growth

YouTube: Love your Enemies by Alexandra McGee –doveinturkey page at YouTube (taught at a camp with just three to four hours of practice)

Solo Exercises:

Play hide and seek with an imaginary friend on the stage: run fast, run slow motion, hide behind walls and squat behind chairs, go in closets, show expression of motivation for each move.

Group Exercises:

In groups of three to five mimes, act out part of a fairy tale skit. Create the skit with a beginning – the problem is set up with the hero having a weakness or flaw; a middle – a struggle over the problem – hero at first fails because of his character flaw; and an end – the battle is won by the hero because he gains mastery over his flaw – but at the same time the hero learns something.

I don't have lessons for mime "tricks" like walking in place or making a wall, because there are plenty of teaching clips on the web. Pat Fenda on e-how has done a terrific job of filming short clips that teach these movements. Early on in our mime troupe, we learned a lot from her videos.

Alexandra McGee, teaching.

<u>Final Thoughts on Movement and Expression in Mime:</u>

While reviewing the principle of "clicks" with my troupe recently, I asked, "How natural is it for you to do clicks?" The mimes who had been with the troupe the longest said it came naturally now. The newer mimes said they have to think about doing clicks or they don't do them at all. It takes effort, concentration and practice to incorporate clicks in your mime acting. But eventually all these principles will become second nature. So keep on miming!

CHAPTER 4
Practices and Performances

I have taken groups who were only with us for two to three weeks from knowing nothing about mime to performing on the street in public four nights a week during their visit with me. The first Romanian troupe we had was asked by audience members how many years they had been performing mime. You can do it too!

Practices

Practices tend to be long: three to four hours. We usually have a break in the middle for snacks. There is also some time for chatting and praying together as well. We have learned that people are whole human beings whose social, spiritual, physical and mental needs should be met; otherwise, they will burn out.

Each practice session usually includes these sections:
1. 15 minutes: Warm up exercises – mostly stretching and some strength training (push- ups, lunges, sit-ups).

2. 1 hour: Improvisation Exercises – short solo and group exercises to learn the principles. I usually teach just one or two principles in a day. The first summer I only taught the first eight principles included in the chapter of exercises. After that I started including some of the more advanced principles, when I had months instead of just weeks to work with a mime troupe.
3. 30 minutes: Break – snack and social time. (Kids need to talk sometimes!)
4. 1 hour: Practice skits we will be performing.
5. 30-60 minutes: Skit creation – playing with new ideas for skits. We don't do this every practice, because sometimes the mimes are just too tired. But some of our best skits have been the product of this creative time.

I use an Excel sheet to organize the practicing of skits. With a troupe of ten, for example, I will try to have them practicing individual skits in groups of two to five mimes at the same time. I will assign myself and the assistant directors to the skits that we are best suited to teach. The assistant directors are usually also in the skit they are directing. Here is an example of how to use an excel sheet to organize your skit practices.

Skit and Mime	M1	M2	M3	M4	M5	M
Skit 1	M2	M2				
Skit 2					M5	M6
Skit 3			M3	M4		
Skit 4	M2	M2	M3	M4	M5	M6

This way you know that you can practice Skit 1,2 and 3 simultaneously (but on different sides of a room or in different rooms), because the mimes are separated out into these skits. Skit 4 requires all the mimes to practice together.

Besides reading through the script, working out the blocking (placement of mimes on the stage), and discussing the feelings and expressions that the mimes will aim for throughout the skit, I'm on the look-out for added touches that come to mind, or that a mime will spontaneously do, to make the skit better. When a troupe is concentrating and excited about mime, they will come up with all sorts of added movements that embellish the skit.

We had one mime who, when playing the "Rich Fool", decided to laugh so hard at the old poor woman he had just kicked out of his house that he shed mime tears and then wiped them with his finger. It was cartoony and very funny. That movement was incorporated into the mime story.

If we have any mimes who are watching other mimes practice, we ask them to give positive feedback. We don't allow critical remarks. We limit these to the director and assistant directors. I look for places where the principles are being broken or for periods when the energy seems low in a skit. Sometimes this is because the mimes are just tired, but it can also be because a mime hasn't understood his part, or because the skit itself is lacking in energy and needs to be revised. Often discussion with the mimes as a group about the skits will help reveal what needs fixing.

Performances:

We have performed both in closed venues on stage as well as on the street where the audience is free to come and go. Our biggest crowds have been on the street. Performing on the street is thrilling because you know that people are standing around watching because they genuinely enjoy the art. We put up a sign that is visible throughout the performance that says "We don't collect money." We do this because we found that otherwise people will sometimes stand at a distance or scatter after each show in fear that we will approach them for money. We have a huge variety of people who will stay and watch, from the corner policeman and the city councilman to the old poor widow and the street urchin. And they are fascinated.

The mimes perform fifteen minute sets of three to five skits each and then take a break to interact with the audience for five to ten minutes.

This gives people a chance to talk to the mimes – and the mimes also play some mime games (volleyball or soccer) with younger kids, make mime balloons for them, take mime pictures, or pick mime flowers. It gives us a chance as well to ask questions and interact with the audience on their thoughts about our skits.

<u>Encouraging Discussion</u>

My husband has developed a social entrepreneurial tool called "Real Love Rocks". It is a love "test" that you can take by accepting a small rock with a heart painted on it and the conditions that go along with the rock. They are: 1.For twenty-four hours, love everyone around you as much as you love yourself.
2. After twenty-four hours pass the rock on to someone else who will do the same. This is our way of encouraging love in the community and starting meaningful conversations that sometimes are the start of long term friendships. You can read more about this at www.RealLoveRocks.org.

Real Love Miming

We have performed with breaks for up to three to four hours when we had really good crowds. It will be exhausting, but some of the most rewarding time you will spend in your life. The audiences often would comment on how joyful the mimes are, how well they work together and how much they love the audiences. This is essential for a truly positive experience.

We encourage the team to love each other, not just when in the public eye, but during the whole time of preparation, rest, and wrap up times after a performance.

Usually we perform two days and then rest one day. We repeat this pattern for the whole time the mimes are in our troupe. On the rest days we take the mimes on special trips to the beach, to tourist spots or shopping.

If we notice attitude or practical difficulties with one of the mimes, we try to deal with this by encouraging positive attitudes, actions or character. A mime who is tired, critical, independent or lazy will have difficulty performing with the troupe effectively.

Practical Tips for Performance:

I (the director) will stand directly in front of the mimes, facing the mimes, while they are performing (about ten feet away). I have cards with pictures on them that I show to the mimes to let them know what the next mime skit is. The audience will almost always gather right behind me and to my sides. The mimes who are not performing will either be standing in a group right behind me, so as not to take up the whole "front row" of the audience, or they will sit if there is an edge on the sides of the "stage" area. This helps establish the stage so that the mimes have room to perform.

All of the mimes and support people who are not in a specific skit watch the performing mimes during the performance. If the non-performing mimes talk to each other or fail to keep their eyes on the performing mimes, it distracts the audience. When we pay attention, we raise the curiosity of those passing by and help them feel comfortable in stopping to watch.

We have titles on signs for some of the skits. These are kept at my feet. A mime that is not in the next skit will grab the sign and walk in a half circle on the stage to show the sign to the whole audience. We will often have a music stand where the title sign will then rest during the time of the skit performance. This must be visible for those who join the audience to watch the mime after a skit has begun. Sometimes, if it is too windy, we have a mime hold up the sign. The title increases the anticipation and understanding of the skit without giving away the whole plot.

I keep a bag of water bottles near me, so that mimes can catch a drink between skits.

It is important that mimes stay in character from the moment you leave the practice hall. In the car on the way to a street venue, they are mimes, so it is very quiet in the car – they might whisper one or two things here and there – but they are focusing on waving at the people who drive by or are on the street walking. When walking from the car to the performance area they are to be silent and walking as mimes – with a bounce in their step. Before, during and after performances, mimes stay continually in character.

Most of the time, mimes do not talk to the audience. But occasionally we make exceptions. But the mime must still stay in mime character while talking. If the spell of wonder is broken, it does more harm to the goodwill of the audience than if you perform poorly.

CHAPTER 5
Make-Up And Costumes

<u>Make-up:</u>

We have found Ben Nye to be a fabulous brand for make-up. The cakes run around $10 for a medium size container that is to be used by one person. They have lasted for a year or longer without going bad. There are many online videos that show how to put the make-up on. It is good if you can create a distinctive design for your troupe make-up. This helps identify you as a unique troupe. All our mimes have hearts on one of their cheeks because our central theme is love.

You will need: white and black cream at least (other colors if you want more designs on your face); white powder to put over the cream; black eye liner; black (for boys) and red (for girls) lipstick; mascara.

<u>Costumes</u>:

We have used two sets of custom-made shirts. Because our mimes perform in sometimes socially conservative countries, we use long sleeve shirts with stripes that also are longish at the waist. This helps prevent any skin showing that might offend viewers.

Each mime wears their own black pants that they bring to the performance as well as their own shoes. We have usually asked that shoes be a solid color: tennis shoes if possible, but plain black shoes are fine too.

We bought black fisherman style hats for all the mimes in our troupe. I have had to periodically buy new sets of gloves online as they get ratty and dirty fairly quickly. I have found polyester blend gloves the best choice, as opposed to 100% cotton, as they wash without shrinking.

Look us up on our websites: <u>heartbeatmime.com</u> and <u>realloverocks.org</u>. You will find scripts for some of our skits there. Let us know what you think of this book and the skits on the ""doveinturkey"" account on YouTube. If you have any questions or want to tell us about your troupe, we would love to correspond with you. May you speak to many hearts as you Mime!

www.ingramcontent.com/pod-product-compliance
Lightning Source LLC
Chambersburg PA
CBHW041535040426
42446CB00002B/100